Phrasebook

EASY ENGLISH

A 1.1

von Oliver Busch

Herausgegeben von Christine House
John Stevens

Easy English A1.1 Phrasebook

Im Auftrag des Verlages erarbeitet von: Oliver Busch

Datenbank und XML: Udo Diekmann
Redaktion: John Stevens
Redaktionelle Mitarbeit: Susanne Schütz, Menemsha MacBain
Tonaufnahme des Aussprachetrainers: James Richardson
Projektleitung: Murdo MacPhail
Gesamtgestaltung und technische Umsetzung: eScriptum GmbH & Co KG, Berlin
Umschlag: Sofarobotnik, Augsburg

www.cornelsen.de

1. Auflage, 1. Druck 2013

Alle Drucke dieser Auflage sind inhaltlich unverändert und können im Unterricht nebeneinander verwendet werden.

© 2013 Cornelsen Schulverlage GmbH, Berlin

Das Werk und seine Teile sind urheberrechtlich geschützt. Jede Nutzung in anderen als den gesetzlich zugelassenen Fällen bedarf der vorherigen schriftlichen Einwilligung des Verlages. Hinweis zu den §§ 46, 52a UrhG: Weder das Werk noch seine Teile dürfen ohne eine solche Einwilligung eingescannt und in ein Netzwerk eingestellt oder sonst öffentlich zugänglich gemacht werden. Das gilt auch für Intranets von Schulen und sonstigen Bildungseinrichtungen.

Druck: H. Heenemann, Berlin

ISBN 978-3-06-520805-5

 Inhalt gedruckt auf säurefreiem Papier aus nachhaltiger Forstwirtschaft.

Einleitung

Im **Easy English A1.1 Phrasebook** können Sie alle Wörter nachschlagen, die in den *Units* des Kursbuches vorkommen. Sie finden zu jedem Wort Hinweise zur Aussprache (Phonetik) und die passende deutsche Übersetzung.

An jeder passenden Stelle in der *Unit*-Wortliste finden Sie außerdem **Phraseboxes**, die nützliche Wörter und Wendungen zusammenfassen, die Sie gut ins Gedächtnis prägen können.

Neben der *Unit*-Wortliste finden Sie im **Easy English A1.1 Phrasebook** auch eine alphabetische Wortliste zum schnellen Nachschlagen einzelner Begriffe, sowie eine Liste von Eigennamen, Ortsnamen, Ländern und Nationalitäten. Mit der Fundstelle bei jedem Eintrag der alphabetischen Liste können Sie das gesuchte Wort schnell in den Texten und Übungen des Kursbuches finden.

Der Aussprachetrainer
Mit der Audio-CD zum **Easy English A1.1 Phrasebook** können Sie zu Hause, im Auto, im Bus oder in der Bahn – also einfach überall, wo Sie einen Moment Zeit haben – die Aussprache des gelernten Vokabulars üben. Entspannen Sie sich, sprechen Sie die Wörter langsam nach und vergewissern Sie sich mit der Übersetzung, dass Sie die Bedeutung verstanden haben.

Tipp
Denken Sie daran, dass es meistens nicht darum geht, jedes einzelne Wort exakt zu verstehen und übersetzen zu können. Versuchen Sie sich die Bedeutungen selbstständig zu erschließen. Überprüfen Sie dann, ob Sie Recht hatten.

Viel Spaß beim Lernen mit Ihrem **Easy English A1.1 Phrasebook**!

Inhalt

Unit word list	S. 5
Alphabetical word list	S. 23
Names, places, countries, nationalities	S. 30

Verwendete Abkürzungen

sb	somebody	jd	jemand	mask	maskulin
sth	something	jdn	jemanden	fem	feminin
so	someone	jdm	jemandem	ugs	umgangssprachlich
swh	somewhere	jds	jemandes		
pl	plural	etw	etwas		
BE	British English				
AE	American English				

Verwendete Symbole

 Hörtext

Hinweise zur Aussprache

ɑː wie in **a**sk [ɑːsk]
ʌ wie in b**u**s [bʌs]
æ wie in c**a**n [kæn]
e wie in **e**nter [ˌentə]
iː wie in h**e** [hiː]
i wie in happ**y** [ˈhæpi]
ɪ wie in s**i**t [sɪt]
ɜː wie in b**i**rthday [ˈbɜːθdeɪ]
ɒ wie in g**o**t [gɒt]
ɔː wie in sh**o**rts [ʃɔːts]
ʊ wie in b**oo**k [bʊk]
uː wie in f**oo**d [fuːd]
u wie in sit**u**ation [ˌsɪtʃuˈeɪʃn]
ə wie in fath**er** [ˈfɑːðə]
aɪ wie in fl**igh**t [flaɪt]
aʊ wie in br**ow**se [ˈbraʊz]
eɪ wie in d**a**te [deɪt]

ɔɪ wie in b**oy** [bɔɪ]
ɪə wie in h**ear** [hɪə]
eə wie in h**air** [heə]
əʊ wie in ph**o**ne [fəʊn]
ʊə wie in s**ure** [ʃʊə]
ŋ wie in darli**ng** [ˈdɑːlɪŋ]
s wie in **s**orry [ˈsɒri]
z wie in **z**ero [ˈzɪərəʊ]
ʃ wie in **sh**op [ʃɒp]
tʃ wie in **ch**icken [ˈtʃɪkɪn]
dʒ wie in **j**ob [dʒɒb]
v wie in **v**ideo [ˈvɪdiəʊ]
r wie in **r**adio [ˈreɪdiəʊ]
ʒ wie in televi**si**on [ˈtelɪvɪʒn]
θ wie in **th**ree [θriː]
ð wie in **th**is [ðɪs]
w wie in **w**onderful [ˈwʌndəfʊl]

Unit 1 Good to meet you!

	good	[gʊd]	gut
	to	[tə, tuː]	zu
	to meet sb	[miːt]	jdn treffen, jdm begegnen, jdn kennen lernen
	Good to meet you!	[ˌgʊd tə ˈmiːt ju]	Schön, Sie/dich/euch kennen zu lernen!
1	to listen	[ˈlɪsn]	zuhören
	and	[ənd]	und
	to repeat	[rɪˈpiːt]	wiederholen
	hi	[haj]	hallo
	hello	[həˈləʊ]	hallo
	my	[maɪ]	mein
	name	[neɪm]	Name
	's = is	[ɪz]	ist
	I	[aɪ]	ich
	I'm = I am	[aɪm, aɪ əm]	ich bin
2	now	[naʊ]	jetzt
	you	[juː]	du, ihr, dich, dir, euch
3	dialogue	[ˈdaɪəlɒg]	Gespräch, Dialog
	are	[ɑː]	bist, sind, seid
	new	[njuː]	neu
	here	[hɪə]	hier
	yes	[jes]	ja
	the	[ðə, ði]	der, die, das
	waitress	[ˈweɪtrɪs]	Kellnerin
	where	[weə]	wo
	from	[frɒm]	aus
	Germany	[ˈdʒɜːməni]	Deutschland
	you're = you are	[jɔ, ju ˌɑː]	du bist, ihr seid, Sie sind
	German	[ˈdʒɜːmən]	Deutsche/r, deutsch, Deutsch
	it	[ɪt]	es
	in	[ɪn]	in
	west	[west]	Westen
	near	[nɪə]	in der Nähe von, nahe
	no	[nəʊ]	nein
	And you.	[ənd ˈjuː]	Ebenfalls., Ebenso.

Good to meet you!

Hi. / Hello. I'm … / My name is …	Hallo. Ich bin / Mein Name ist …
This is … She is the new waitress.	Das ist … Sie ist die neue Kellnerin.
Are you new here?	Sind Sie / bist du / seid ihr neu hier?
Good to meet you. –And you.	Schön, Sie / dich / euch kennenzulernen. – Gleichfalls.
Sorry, I must go.	Tut mir leid, ich muss gehen.
See you again. / Goodbye.	Auf Wiedersehen.

	Great Britain	[ˌgreɪt 'brɪtn]	Großbritannien
	England	['ɪŋglənd]	England
	Scotland	['skɑtlənd]	Schottland
	Wales	[welz]	Wales
	Northern Ireland	['nɔrðərn 'ajərlənd]	Nordirland
	Ireland	['aɪələnd]	Irland
4	quick	[kwɪk]	schnell
	check	[tʃek]	Überprüfung, Kontrolle
5	language	['læŋgwɪdʒ]	Sprache
6	practice	['præktɪs]	Praxis, Übung, Training
8	word	[wɜːd]	Wort
	north	[nɔːθ]	Norden
	south	[saʊθ]	Süden
	east	[iːst]	Osten

Where are you from?

Are you from near here?	Kommen Sie / kommst du / kommt ihr hier aus der Nähe?
Are you from …?	Kommen Sie / kommst du / kommt ihr aus …?
I'm from …	Ich komme aus …
It's in the north/east/west/south.	Das ist im Norden / Osten / Süden / Westen.
It's near …	Das ist in der Nähe von …

	Austria	['ɒstriə]	Österreich
	Switzerland	['swɪtsələnd]	Schweiz
	Cologne	[kə'ləʊn]	Köln
	Munich	['mjuːnɪk]	München
	Vienna	[vi'enə]	Wien
10	pronunciation	[prəˌnʌnsi'eɪʃn]	Aussprache
11	round up	['raʊnd ʌp]	Zusammenfassung

Unit 2 This is …

	this	[ðɪs]	diese/r/s, dies, das
1	airport	['eəpɔːt]	Flughafen
	book	[bʊk]	Buch

	shop	[ʃɒp]	Laden, Geschäft
	bookshop	['bʊk ʃɒp]	Buchhandlung
	café	['kæfeɪ]	Café
	car	[kɑː]	Auto
	car park	['kɑː pɑːk]	Parkplatz, Parkhaus, Tiefgarage
	check-in	['tʃekɪn]	Abfertigung(sschalter), Check-in
	duty-free	['duti fri]	zollfrei
	gate	[geɪt]	Flugsteig, Gate
	hotel	[həʊ'tel]	Hotel
	information	[ˌɪnfə'meɪʃn]	Auskunft, Information(en)
	lift	[lɪft]	Aufzug, Fahrstuhl, Lift
	pub	[pʌb]	Kneipe
	reception	[rɪ'sepʃn]	Empfang, Rezeption
	restaurant	['restrɒnt]	Restaurant
	toilet	['tɔɪlət]	Toilette

Where are you?

Are you in the cafe / at the gate? Sind Sie/bist du / seid ihr im Café / am Flugsteig?
– Yes, I am. / No, I'm not. – Ja(, bin ich). / Nein(, bin ich nicht).
Is he in the pub? Ist er in der Kneipe?
– Yes, he is. / No, he's not. – Ja(, ist er). / Nein(, ist er nicht).

4	or	[ɔː]	oder
	barman	['bɑːmən]	Barmann, Barkeeper
	at	[æt]	in, bei, an
	Irish	['aɪrɪʃ]	irisch, Ire/Irin
	Australia	[ɒ'streɪliə]	Australien
	sorry	['sɒri]	Entschuldigung!, Tut mir Leid!
	must	[mʌst]	müssen
	to go	[gəʊ]	gehen
	nice	[naɪs]	schön, nett, gut
	to see	[siː]	sehen
	again	[ə'gen]	wieder
	See you again.	[ˌsiː ju ə'gen]	auf Wiedersehen
	goodbye	[ˌgʊd'baɪ]	auf Wiedersehen
	bye	[baɪ]	tschüs
	he	[hiː]	er
5	she	[ʃiː]	sie
6	not	[nɒt]	nicht
9	listening	['lɪsnɪŋ]	Zuhören

Unit 3 Cheers!

	Cheers!	[tʃɪəz]	Prost!
	a	[ə, eɪ]	ein/e/r/s
	glass	[glɑːs]	Glas

1	of	[əv]	von, aus
	red	[red]	rot
	wine	[waɪn]	Wein
	red wine	[ˌred ˈwaɪn]	Rotwein
	please	[pliːz]	bitte
	water	[ˈwɔːtə]	Wasser
	orange	[ˈɒrɪndʒ]	orange, Apfelsine
	juice	[dʒuːs]	Saft
	white	[waɪt]	weiß
	bottle	[ˈbɒtl]	Flasche
	Here you are.	[ˌhɪə ju ˈɑː]	Bitte (schön)., Hier, bitte.

At the bar

– It's my round. What would you like? — Die Runde geht auf mich. Was hätten Sie / hättest du / hättet ihr gern?

A pint of bitter, please. — Ein Pint halbdunkles Ale vom Fass, bitte.
– Is that all? — Ist das alles?
No, a bottle of beer and a glass of water, please. — Nein, eine Flasche Bier und ein Glas Wasser, bitte.
– Here you are. — Bitte(schön).
We can drink to the good old days. Cheers! — Wir können auf die gute alte Zeit anstoßen. Prost!

3	student	[ˈstjuːdnt]	Schüler/in
	beer	[bɪə]	Bier
	teacher	[ˈtiːtʃə]	Lehrer/in
4	how	[haʊ]	wie
	How are you?	[ˌhaʊ ə ˈjuː]	Wie geht es dir/euch/Ihnen?
	today	[təˈdeɪ]	heute
	woman	[ˈwʊmən]	Frau
	fine	[faɪn]	gut, schön
	I'm fine.	[aɪm ˈfaɪn]	Mit geht es gut.
	thanks	[θæŋks]	danke
	day	[deɪ]	Tag
	bad	[bæd]	schlecht, schlimm
6	that	[ðæt]	der, die, das, diese/r/s, jene/r/s
	all	[ɔːl]	alle, alles
	too	[tuː]	auch, noch dazu
	we	[wiː]	wir
	me	[miː]	ich, mir, mich
	Me too.	[ˌmiː ˈtuː]	Ich auch.
	great	[greɪt]	toll, prima, großartig
	place	[pleɪs]	Ort
	but	[bʌt]	aber
	both	[bəʊθ]	beide
	very	[ˈveri]	sehr
	there	[ðeə]	dort, da

	they	[ðeɪ]	sie
8	man	[mæn]	Mann

How are you?

And how are you today?	Wie geht es Ihnen / dir / euch heute?
Nice day today.	Schöner Tag heute.
Yes it is. / Yes, it's not bad.	Ja, das ist es. / Ja, nicht schlecht.
Are you both from …? Me too.	Sind Sie / seid ihr beide aus …? Ich auch.
That's a nice place.	Dort ist es sehr schön.

Unit 4 An espresso, please

1	an	[ən]	ein/e/r/s
	chocolate	['tʃɒklət]	Schokolade
	coffee	['kɒfi]	Kaffee
	drink	[drɪŋk]	Getränk
	self service	[ˌself 'sɜːvɪs]	Selbstbedienung
	snack	[snæk]	Imbiss
	tea	[tiː]	Tee
2	What about you?	[ˌwɒt əbaʊt 'juː]	Was ist mit dir/euch/Ihnen?
	cup	[kʌp]	Tasse
	a cup of tea	[ə ˌkʌp əf 'tiː]	eine Tasse Tee
	piece	[piːs]	Stück
	cheese	[tʃiːz]	Käse
	cake	[keɪk]	Torte, Kuchen
	cheesecake	['tʃiːzkeɪk]	Käsekuchen
	milk	[mɪlk]	Milch
	for	[fə, fɔː]	für
	little	['lɪtl]	klein
	boy	[bɔɪ]	Junge
	girl	[gɜːl]	Mädchen
	hungry	['hʌŋgri]	hungrig
	to be hungry	[bi 'hʌŋgri]	Hunger haben

In the café

Drinks for you? – No, thank you. What about you?	Etwas zu trinken für Sie / dich / euch? – Nein, danke. Was ist mit dir / euch / Ihnen?
What about a drink? – That's a good idea.	Wie wäre es mit einem Getränk? – Das ist eine gute Idee.
I'm hungry. Two cream teas, please.	Ich habe Hunger. Zwei Tee mit Scones, bitte.
The espresso is for me, please.	Der Espresso ist für mich, bitte.

	magic word	[ˌmædʒɪk 'wɜːd]	Zauberwort
	better	['betə]	besser

	one	[wʌn]	ein/e, eins
	so	[səʊ]	also
	two	[tuː]	zwei
	three	[θriː]	drei
	four	[fɔː]	vier
	thank you	['θæŋk juː]	danke
5	then	[ðen]	dann
9	five	[faɪv]	fünf
	six	[sɪks]	sechs
	seven	['sevn]	sieben
	eight	[eɪt]	acht
	nine	[naɪn]	neun
	ten	[ten]	zehn

Unit 5 Consolidation

	consolidation	[kənˌsɒlɪ'deɪʃn]	Vertiefung, Festigung
2	Austrian	['ɒstriən]	österreichisch, Österreicher/in
	Swiss	[swɪs]	schweizerisch, Schweizer/in
	Britain	['brɪtn]	Britannien
	British	['brɪtɪʃ]	britisch, Brite/Britin
	English	['ɪŋglɪʃ]	englisch, Engländer/in
	Australian	[ɒ'streɪliən]	australisch, Australier/in
3	flag	[flæg]	Flagge
	number	['nʌmbə]	Nummer
	colour	['kʌlə]	Farbe
	What colour is …?	[ˌwɒt 'kʌlər ɪz]	Welche Farbe hat …?
	blue	[bluː]	blau
4	green	[griːn]	grün
	yellow	['jeləʊ]	gelb
	black	[blæk]	schwarz
	orange	['ɒrɪndʒ]	orange
	purple	['pɜːpl]	lila, violett

Colours

What colour is …? – It's …	Welche Farbe hat …? … ist …
… red	… rot
… blue	… blau
… green	… grün
… yellow	… gelb
… pink	… rosa
… black	… schwarz
… orange	… orange
… purple	… lila
… grey	… grau
… brown	… braun

	pink	[pɪŋk]	rosa
	grey	[greɪ]	grau
	brown	[braʊn]	braun
6	to fill in	[ˌfɪl 'ɪn]	ausfüllen, ergänzen

Unit 6 Let's keep in touch

	to let	[let]	lassen

Asking for a name

What's your name / first name / surname? — Wie ist Ihr / dein / euer Name / Vorname / Familienname?
Can you spell that, please? — Können Sie / kannst du / könnt ihr das bitte buchstabieren?
Let's keep in touch! — Lassen Sie uns / lass uns / lasst uns in Verbindung bleiben.

	to keep in touch	[ˌkiːp ɪn 'tʌtʃ]	in Verbindung bleiben
1	your	[jɔː]	dein, euer, Ihr
	phone	[fəʊn]	Telefon
	right	[raɪt]	richtig
	That's right.	[ˌðəts 'raɪt]	Das stimmt, Das ist richtig.
3	home	[həʊm]	Heim, Zuhause, Haus, Wohnung
	mobile	['məʊbaɪl]	Mobiltelefon, Handy
	can	[kæn]	können
	to say	[seɪ]	sagen
	again	[ə'gen]	noch einmal
	to have	[həv, hæv]	haben
	address	[ə'dres]	Adresse, Anschrift

Asking for a phone number / an address

What's your mobile / home number? – It's … — Wie ist Ihre / deine / eure Handynummer / Festnetznummer? – Sie lautet …
So that's … – That's right. — Also … – Das stimmt.
Can I have your home address, please? — Kann ich bitte Ihre / deine / eure Privatadresse haben?
Can I check that / Can you say that again, please? — Kann ich das überprüfen / Können Sie / kannst du / könnt ihr das bitte wiederholen?

	of course	[əf 'kɔːs]	natürlich, selbstverständlich
	postcode	['pəʊstkəʊd]	Postleitzahl
	to check	[tʃek]	überprüfen, kontrollieren
	surname	['sɜːneɪm]	Nachname
9	with	[wɪð, wɪθ]	mit

dot	[dɒt]	Punkt
to spell	[spel]	buchstabieren
first name	['fɜːst neɪm]	Vorname

On the phone

Hello. It's …	Hallo. Hier ist …
Is that … / Can I speak to …, please?	Ist da … / Kann ich bitte mit … sprechen?
Is that a good time?	Passt es gerade?
I can text you.	Ich kann Ihnen / dir / euch eine SMS schicken.

Unit 7 Have a good flight!

	flight	[flaɪt]	Flug
1	boarding pass	['bɔːdɪŋ pɑːs]	Bordkarte
	boarding card	['bɔːdɪŋ kɑːd]	Bordkarte
	time	[taɪm]	Zeit
	boarding time	['bɔːdɪŋ taɪm]	Einsteigezeit

At the airport

He is at …	Er ist beim / bei der / bei den …
… the baggage reclaim	… Gepäckausgabe
… passports	… Passkontrolle
… customs	… Zoll
… car rental	… Autovermietung
… arrivals	… Ankünften
… exit	… Ausgang
… flight connections	… im Transitbereich

	date	[deɪt]	Datum
	passenger	['pæsɪndʒə]	Passagier
	passport	['pɑːspɔːt]	Reisepass
	seat	[siːt]	Platz, Sitz
2	to read	[riːd]	lesen
	his	[hɪz]	sein
	on	[ɒn]	auf, an, bei
	her	[hɜː]	ihr
3	shop assistant	['ʃɒp əsɪstənt]	Verkäufer/in
	sir	[sɜː]	mein Herr
	sure	[ʃʊə]	sicher
	all right	[ɔːl 'raɪt]	in Ordnung
	to	[tə, tuː]	nach
	credit card	['kredɪt kɑːd]	Kreditkarte
	to sign	[saɪn]	unterschreiben

	Excuse me.	[ɪk'skjuːz mi]	Entschuldigung!
	Pardon?	['pɑːdn]	Wie bitte?
	much	[mʌtʃ]	viel
	thank you very much	[ˌθæŋk ju ˌveri 'mʌtʃ]	vielen Dank
	welcome	['welkəm]	willkommen
	You're welcome.	[jɔː 'welkəm]	Bitte sehr., Gern geschehen.
8	job	[dʒɒb]	Arbeit, Stelle

In the duty-free shop

What's your flight number, sir?	Wie ist Ihre Flugnummer(, mein Herr)?
Excuse me. – Pardon?	Entschuldigung. – Wie bitte?
Can you sign here, please?	Können Sie bitte hier unterschreiben?
Thank you very much. – You're welcome.	Vielen Dank. – Sehr gerne.
Have a good flight!	Guten Flug!

Unit 8 What's the town like?

	town	[taʊn]	Stadt
	like	[laɪk]	wie
1	far	[fɑː]	weit (entfernt)
	there is/are	['ðeər ɪz/ɑː]	es gibt
	bus	[bʌs]	Bus
	train	[treɪn]	Zug
3	bank	[bæŋk]	Bank
	normal	['nɔːml]	normal, gewöhnlich
	thing	[θɪŋ]	Ding, Sache
	centre	['sentə]	Zentrum
	shopping centre	['ʃɒpɪŋ sentə]	Einkaufszentrum
	out of sth	['aʊt əv]	außerhalb von etw
	what else?	[ˌwɒt 'els]	was noch?
	theatre	['θɪətə]	Theater
	person	['pɜːsn]	Person, Mensch
	a theatre person	[ə 'θɪətə pɜːsn]	jd, der gern ins Theater geht
	many	['meni]	viele
	interesting	['ɪntrəstɪŋ]	interessant
	big	[bɪɡ]	groß
	city	['sɪti]	Stadt
	tour	[tʊə]	Rundfahrt
	to do	[duː]	tun, machen
	idea	[aɪ'dɪə]	Gedanke, Idee
5	church	[tʃɜːtʃ]	Kirche
	cinema	['sɪnəmə]	Kino
	museum	[mjuˈziːəm]	Museum
	restaurant	['restrɒnt]	Restaurant
	cathedral	[kə'θiːdrəl]	Dom, Kathedrale

What's the town like?

Where's …? – It isn't very far.	Wo liegt …? – Das ist nicht sehr weit weg.
Is there a bus from here? – Yes, there is. / No, there isn't.	Gibt es einen Bus von hier aus? – Ja, den gibt es. / Nein, den gibt es nicht.
What's the town like? – It's ok. There are all the normal things.	Wie ist die Stadt denn so? – Sie ist ganz in Ordnung. Es gibt alles, was man so braucht.
Is there a …? – Yes, there is one out of town.	Gibt es dort einen / eine / ein …? – Ja, es gibt einen / eine / eins außerhalb der Stadt.
And what else is there?	Und was gibt es dort sonst noch?
Sorry, I'm not a theatre person.	Tut mir leid, ich bin niemand, die / der gerne ins Theater geht.

post office	[ˈpəʊst ˌɒfɪs]	Postamt
swimming pool	[ˈswɪmɪŋ puːl]	Schwimmbad
10 modern	[ˈmɒdn]	modern
art	[ɑːt]	Kunst
gallery	[ˈɡæləri]	Galerie, Museum
other	[ˈʌðə]	andere/r/s

Unit 9 It's a great place!

Visiting a city

What can we do today? – We can …	Was können wir heute machen? Wir können …
… go for a walk in the park.	… im Park spazieren gehen.
… go shopping.	… einkaufen gehen.
… go to a waterfront café.	… in ein Café im Hafenviertel gehen.
… take a bus tour.	… eine Stadtrundfahrt machen.
… see a museum.	… ein Museum besichtigen.

1	to go shopping	[ˌɡəʊ ˈʃɒpɪŋ]	einkaufen gehen
	to have sth	[hæv]	etw essen, etw trinken, etw (zu sich) nehmen
	waterfront	[ˈwɔːtəfrʌnt]	Hafen, Hafenviertel
	on the waterfront	[ɒn ðə ˈwɔːtəfrʌnt]	am Wasser, im Hafen
	to see sth	[siː]	etw besichtigen
	to visit	[ˈvɪzɪt]	besuchen, besichtigen
	walk	[wɔːk]	Spaziergang
	to go for a walk	[ˌɡəʊ fər ə ˈwɔːk]	spazieren gehen
2	Dear …	[dɪə]	Liebe/r (Brief:)
	old	[əʊld]	alt
	to take	[teɪk]	nehmen
	in one day	[ɪn ˌwʌn ˈdeɪ]	innerhalb eines Tages, an einem (einzigen) Tag

friendly	['frendli]	freundlich
always	['ɔːlweɪz]	immer

On a bus tour

You can't see all in one day.   Man kann nicht alles an einem Tag besichtigen.
You can have a tour for two hours in   Sie können eine zweistündige Stadtrundfahrt in
the comfort of our bus.   unseren komfortablen Bussen machen.
Groups of 6 people are £45.   Gruppen mit 6 Personen kosten £45.

	to **understand**	[ˌʌndə'stænd]	verstehen
	people *(pl)*	['piːpl]	Personen, Menschen, Leute
	their	[ðeə]	ihr/e
	best	[best]	beste/r/s
	wish	[wɪʃ]	Wunsch
	Best wishes *(pl)*	[ˌbest 'wɪʃɪz]	Herzliche Grüße *(Brief:)*
8	**welcome to** sb/sth	['welkəm]	willkommen bei jdm/etw
	childhood	['tʃaɪldhʊd]	Kindheit
	more	[mɔː]	mehr
	to **come**	[kʌm]	kommen
	our	['aʊə]	unser
	magical	['mædʒɪkl]	magisch, traumhaft
	mystery tour	['mɪstri tʊə]	Entdeckungsreise, Fahrt ins Blaue
	comfort	['kʌmfət]	Komfort
	luxury	['lʌkʃəri]	Luxus
	five-seater	[ˌfaɪv 'siːtə]	Fünfsitzer
	taxi-cab	['tæksɪkæb]	Taxi
	group	[gruːp]	Gruppe
	hour	['aʊə]	Stunde
	price	[praɪs]	Preis
10	**past**	[paːst]	nach
	to	[tə, tuː]	vor
	o'clock	[ə'klɒk]	Uhr
	half past six	[ˌhaːf paːst 'sɪks]	halb sieben
	a quarter past/to	[ə 'kwɔːtə paːst/tə]	Viertel nach/vor
11	**What time is it?**	[wɒt 'taɪm ɪz ɪt]	Wieviel Uhr ist es?, Wie spät ist es?

What number is …?

What time is the bus to Liverpool?   Um wie viel Uhr fährt der Bus nach Liverpool?
– Here's a bus at twenty-five to ten.   – Hier fährt ein Bus um fünf nach halb zehn.
What number is it?   Welche Nummer hat er?
– It's number thirteen.   – Nummer dreizehn.

Unit 10 Consolidation

1	national	[[ˈnæʃnəl]]	national, National-
	tower	[ˈtaʊə]	Turm
	eye	[aɪ]	Auge
	science	[ˈsaɪəns]	Naturwissenschaft
	top	[tɒp]	oberste/r/s, Spitzen-
2	sight	[saɪt]	Sehenswürdigkeit
	attraction	[əˈtrækʃn]	Attraktion
	famous	[ˈfeɪməs]	berühmt
	building	[ˈbɪldɪŋ]	Gebäude
	garden	[ˈgɑːdn]	Garten, Park
	bus stop	[ˈbʌs stɒp]	Bushaltestelle
	gym	[dʒɪm]	Fitnessstudio
	hospital	[ˈhɒspɪtl]	Krankenhaus
3	well	[wel]	nun, nun ja
🔊 56	What about …?	[ˈwɒt əbaʊt]	Wie wäre es mit …?
9	Monday	[ˈmʌndeɪ]	Montag
	Tuesday	[ˈtjuːzdeɪ]	Dienstag
	Wednesday	[ˈwenzdeɪ]	Mittwoch
	Thursday	[ˈθɜːzdeɪ]	Donnerstag
	Friday	[ˈfraɪdeɪ]	Freitag
	Saturday	[ˈsætədeɪ]	Samstag
	Sunday	[ˈsʌndeɪ]	Sonntag
10	on Thursday	[ɒn ˈθɜːzdeɪ]	am Donnerstag
	open	[ˈəʊpən]	offen, geöffnet
	am	[ˌeɪ ˈem]	vor 12 Uhr mittags
	pm	[ˌpiː ˈem]	nach 12 mittags
11	friend	[frend]	Freund/in

Opening hours

The shop is open …
… from 9.00 am – 5.30 pm.
… on Saturday and Sunday.
… Monday to Friday.
We're closed on Wednesday, Thursday and Friday.

Das Geschäft ist …
… von 9.00 – 17.30 Uhr geöffnet.
… am Samstag und Sonntag geöffnet.
… von Montag bis Freitag geöffnet.
Mittwoch, Donnerstag und Freitag haben wir geschlossen.

Unit 11 Enjoy your meal!

	to enjoy	[ɪnˈdʒɔɪ]	genießen
	meal	[miːl]	Mahlzeit, Essen
	Enjoy your meal!	[ɪnˌdʒɔɪ jə ˈmiːl]	Guten Appetit!
1	to like	[laɪk]	mögen

	meat	[miːt]	Fleisch
	really	['riːəli]	wirklich, tatsächlich
	vegetarian	[ˌvedʒə'teəriən]	Vegetarier/in
	to eat	[iːt]	essen
3	a pity	[ə 'pɪti]	schade
	why	[waɪ]	warum
	because	[bɪ'kɒz]	weil
	beef	[biːf]	Rindfleisch
	roast beef	['rəʊst biːf]	Rinderbraten
	traditional	[trə'dɪʃənl]	traditionell
	lunch	[lʌntʃ]	Mittagessen
	menu	['menjuː]	Speisekarte
	soup	[suːp]	Suppe
	a lot of	[ə 'lɒt əv]	viel
	chips	[tʃɪps]	Pommes frites
	to drink	[drɪŋk]	trinken
	lunchtime	['lʌntʃtaɪm]	Mittagszeit
	at lunchtime	['lʌntʃtaɪm]	zur Mittagszeit

Enjoy your meal!

Can I see the menu, please?	Könnte ich bitte die Karte sehen?
I like / eat ... but I don't like / eat ...	Ich mag / esse gern..., aber ich mag kein / esse nicht gern ...
I have a snack for breakfast / lunch / dinner.	Zum Frühstück / Mittagessen / Abendessen esse ich eine Kleinigkeit.
I don't drink at lunchtime.	Ich trinke zur Mittagszeit noch keinen Alkohol.
Ok, fish for you and beef for me.	O. K., für Sie / dich / euch Fisch und für mich Fleisch.
That's a traditional Sunday lunch.	Das ist ein traditionelles Sonntagsessen.
Enjoy your meal!	Guten Appetit!

	Go on.	[ˌgəʊ 'ɒn]	Komm schon!
	to think	[θɪŋk]	denken, glauben, finden
	food	[fuːd]	Essen
	waiter	['weɪtə]	Kellner
	lady	['leɪdi]	Dame
8	breakfast	['brekfəst]	Frühstück
	for lunch	[fə 'lʌntʃ]	zum Mittagessen
	main	[meɪn]	Haupt-
	dinner	['dɪnə]	Abendessen
	hot	[hɒt]	heiß, warm
9	evening	['iːvnɪŋ]	Abend
	in the evening	[ɪn ðɪ 'iːvnɪŋ]	am Abend, abends

Unit 12 I sing in the bath

	to sing	[sɪŋ]	singen
	bath	[bɑːθ]	Badewanne
1	gardening	['gɑːdnɪŋ]	Gärtnern, Gartenarbeit
	dancing	['dɑːnsɪŋ]	Tanzen
	walking	['wɔːkɪŋ]	Spazierengehen
	swimming	['swɪmɪŋ]	Schwimmen
	to meet sb	[miːt]	sich mit jdm treffen
	to play	[pleɪ]	spielen
	to watch	[wɒtʃ]	sehen, ansehen
	TV	[ˌtiː 'viː]	Fernseher, Fernsehen
	to watch TV	[wɒtʃ ˌtiː'viː]	fernsehen
2	free	[friː]	frei
	free time	[ˌfriː 'taɪm]	Freizeit
	cookery	['kʊkəri]	Kochen
	programme	['prəʊgræm]	Sendung
	cookery programme	['kʊkəri prəʊgræm]	Kochsendung
	to cook	[kʊk]	kochen
	at home	[ət 'həʊm]	zu Hause
	when	[wen]	wann
	after	['ɑːftə]	nach
	work	[wɜːk]	Arbeit
	relaxing	[rɪ'læksɪŋ]	entspannend
	class	[klɑːs]	Kurs
	evening class	['iːvnɪŋ klɑːs]	Abendkurs

What do you do?

What do you do in your free time? Was machen Sie / machst du / macht ihr in ihrer / deiner / eurer Freizeit?
I do … – Really? Me too. Ich mache … – Wirklich? Ich auch.
When do you do that? Wann machen Sie / machst du / macht ihr das?
– After work. – Nach der Arbeit.
Where do you do that? Wo machen Sie / machst du / macht ihr das?
– I go to evening classes. – Ich gehe zu Abendkursen.
That's interesting / nice. Das ist interessant / schön.

	choir	['kwaɪə]	Chor
	husband	['hʌzbənd]	(Ehe-)Mann
	where	[weə]	wohin
	to love	[lʌv]	lieben, sehr mögen
	to dance	[dɑːns]	tanzen
8	film	[fɪlm]	Film
9	sports	[spɔːts]	Sport
10	weekend	[ˌwiːk'end]	Wochenende
	at the weekend	[ət ðə ˌwiːk'end]	am Wochenende, wochenends

night	[naɪt]	Abend, Nacht
at night	[ət 'naɪt]	abends, nachts
morning	['mɔ:nɪŋ]	Morgen
afternoon	[ˌɑ:ftə'nu:n]	Nachmittag

Unit 13 How much is it?

	how	[haʊ]	wie
	How much is/are …?	[ˌhaʊ 'mʌtʃ ɪz/ɑ:]	Wieviel kostet/n …?
1	It says …	[ɪt 'sez]	Hier steht …
	euro	['jʊərəʊ]	Euro
	to know	[nəʊ]	wissen
	It doesn't say.	[ɪt ˌdʌznt 'seɪ]	Das steht hier nicht.
3	present	['preznt]	Geschenk
	clothes *(pl)*	[kləʊðz]	Kleider, Kleidung

Buying clothes

What about this sweater? – I think it's lovely.	Wie wäre es mit diesem Pullover? – Ich finde, der ist hübsch.
Let's buy it for you. – Is it a good colour for me?	Lassen Sie ihn uns / lass ihn uns / lasst ihn uns für Sie / dich / euch kaufen. – Steht mir die Farbe gut?
Would you like it? – Oh yes please!	Würden Sie / würdest du / würdet ihr ihn gerne haben? – Oh ja, bitte!
What's the problem? – The colour doesn't look very nice.	Gibt es ein Problem? – Die Farbe sieht nicht sehr schön aus.
That's real … It looks perfect!	Das ist echte / echter / echtes … Das sieht perfekt aus!

game	[geɪm]	Spiel
to sell	[sel]	verkaufen
sweater	['swetə]	Pullover
to cost	[kɒst]	kosten
too	[tu:]	zu
too much	[ˌtu: 'mʌtʃ]	zu viel

How much is it?

How much is / are …? -I don't know. / It says …	Wie viel kostet / kosten …? -Ich weiß nicht. / Hier steht …
That's too much! / That's OK.	Das ist zu viel! / Das ist o. k.
What's that in dollars? – It doesn't say.	Wie viel ist das in Dollar? – Das steht hier nicht.

		real	[rɪəl]	echt
		cashmere	[ˈkæʃmɪə]	Kaschmir, Kaschmirwolle
		soccer	[ˈsɒkə]	Fußball
		to live	[lɪv]	leben, wohnen
		to want	[wɒnt]	wollen
		to buy	[baɪ]	kaufen
		size	[saɪz]	Größe
		you're right	[jɔː ˈraɪt]	du hast Recht
		lovely	[ˈlʌvli]	hübsch, nett, wunderbar
		to look	[lʊk]	aussehen
		perfect	[ˈpɜːfɪkt]	perfekt
		would	[wʊd]	würde
	8	fruit	[fruːt]	Obst, Früchte
	9	pence *(pl)*	[pens]	Pence *(Plural von penny:)*
		pound	[paʊnd]	Pfund
		note BE	[nəʊt]	Geldschein
		bill AE	[bɪl]	Geldschein
	10	only	[ˈəʊnli]	nur
9	72	hundred	[ˈhʌndrəd]	hundert
		ma'am	[mæm]	gnädige Frau
	11	toy	[tɔɪ]	Spielzeug
		shirt	[ʃɜːt]	Hemd
		football	[ˈfʊtbɔːl]	Fußball
		football shirt	[ˈfʊtbɔːl ʃɜːt]	Fußballtrikot

Unit 14 Where does your son live?

		son	[sʌn]	Sohn
	1	brother	[ˈbrʌðə]	Bruder
		father	[ˈfɑːðə]	Vater
		granddaughter	[ˈgrændɔːtə]	Enkelin
		grandmother	[ˈgrænmʌðə]	Großmutter
		partner	[ˈpɑːtnə]	Partner/in, Lebensgefährte/-in
		wife	[waɪf]	(Ehe-)Frau

My family

Here's a photo of my …	Hier ist ein Foto von meinem/meiner …
… husband / wife	… (Ehe-)Mann / (Ehe-)Frau
… father / mother	… Vater / Mutter
… grandfather / grandmother	… Großvater / Großmutter
… brother / sister	… Bruder / Schwester
… son / daughter	… Sohn / Tochter
… uncle / aunt	… Onkel / Tante
… nephew / niece	… Neffen / Nichte
… grandson / granddaughter	… Enkel/in
… partner	… Partner/in

mother	[ˈmʌðə]	Mutter
grandfather	[ˈɡrænfɑːðə]	Großvater
daughter	[ˈdɔːtə]	Tochter
grandson	[ˈɡrænsʌn]	Enkel
sister	[ˈsɪstə]	Schwester

3 flight attendant [ˈflaɪt ətendənt] Flugbegleiter/in
   to work [wɜːk] arbeiten

Work

Where does ... work? / Does ... work for ...?   Wo arbeitet ...? / Arbeitet ... für/bei ...?
What does ... do? – ... is a ...   Was macht (beruflich)? – ... ist ...
... *pilot / flight attendant*   ... Pilot/in / Flugbegleiter/in
... *cook / barman*   ... Koch/Köchin / Barkeeper/in
... *teacher / kindergarten teacher*   ... Lehrer/in / Kindergärtner/in
... *shop assistant*   ... Verkäufer/in
... *policeman*   ... Polizist/in
... *astronaut*   ... Astronaut/in
... *footballer*   ... Fußballspieler/in
... *secretary*   ... Sekretär/in

airline	[ˈeəlaɪn]	Fluggesellschaft
just	[dʒʌst]	nur, gerade
Just a minute.	[ˌdʒʌst ə ˈmɪnɪt]	Moment mal., Einen Moment.
photo	[ˈfəʊtəʊ]	Foto
to miss	[mɪs]	vermissen
who	[huː]	wer
married to sb	[ˈmærɪd]	mit jdm verheiratet
a lot	[ə ˈlɒt]	viel, oft
cook	[kʊk]	Koch/Köchin
kindergarten teacher	[ˈkɪndəɡɑːtn tiːtʃə]	Kindergärtner/in
footballer	[ˈfʊtbɔːlə]	Fußballspieler/in
policeman	[pəˈliːsmən]	Polizist
pilot	[ˈpaɪlət]	Pilot/in
astronaut	[ˈæstrənɔːt]	Astronaut/in
only	[ˈəʊnli]	erst
I see.	[ˌaɪ ˈsiː]	Verstehe., Ah ja.
10 sport	[spɔːt]	Sport
point	[pɔɪnt]	Punkt
team	[tiːm]	Mannschaft

Unit 15 Consolidation

1	secretary	[ˈsekrətri]	Sekretär/in
	company	[ˈkʌmpəni]	Firma, Unternehmen
	to drive	[draɪv]	fahren

office	['ɒfɪs]	Büro
downtown	['daʊntaʊn]	in der/die Innenstadt
every	['evri]	jede/r/s
sometimes	['sʌmtaɪmz]	manchmal
retired	[rɪ'taɪəd]	im Ruhestand
mile	[maɪl]	Meile
parents *(pl)*	['peərənts]	Eltern
often	['ɒfn]	oft
3 family	['fæməli]	Familie
10 tuna fish	['tjuːnə fɪʃ]	Thunfisch

Alphabetical word list

In der folgenden Liste finden Sie die Einträge der Unit-Liste in alphabetischer Reihenfolge. Die Bestandteile von Einträgen, die aus mehreren Wörtern bestehen, sind auch unter ihren jeweiligen Anfangsbuchstaben zu finden (ausgenommen Präpositionen oder ähnliche Funktionswörter). Beispiel: Aus dem Eintrag a *cup of tea*, der unter ‚A' aufgelistet ist, finden Sie sowohl *cup* unter ‚C' als auch *tea* unter ‚T'.

A

a 3/ ein/e/r/s
a cup of tea 4/2 eine Tasse Tee
address 6/3 Adresse, Anschrift
after 12/2 nach
afternoon 12/10 Nachmittag
again 2/4 wieder
again 6/3 noch einmal
airline 14/3 Fluggesellschaft
airport 2/1 Flughafen
all 3/6 alle, alles
all right 7/3 in Ordnung
a lot 14/3 viel, oft
a lot of 11/3 viel
always 9/2 immer
am 10/10 vor 12 Uhr mittags
an 4/ ein/e/r/s
and 1/1 und
And you. 1/3 Ebenfalls., Ebenso.
a pity 11/3 schade
a quarter past/to 9/10 Viertel nach/vor
are 1/3 bist, sind, seid
art 8/10 Kunst
astronaut 14/3 Astronaut/in
at 2/4 in, bei, an
a theatre person 8/3 jd, der gern ins Theater geht
at home 12/2 zu Hause
at lunchtime 11/3 zur Mittagszeit
at night 12/10 abends, nachts
at the weekend 12/10 am Wochenende, wochenends

attraction 10/2 Attraktion
Australia 2/4 Australien
Australian 5/2 australisch, Australier/in
Austria 1/8 Österreich
Austrian 5/2 österreichisch, Österreicher/in

B

bad 3/4 schlecht, schlimm
bank 8/3 Bank
barman 2/4 Barmann, Barkeeper
bath 12/ Badewanne
because 11/3 weil
beef 11/3 Rindfleisch
beer 3/3 Bier
best 9/2 beste/r/s
Best wishes (pl) 9/2 Herzliche Grüße
better 4/2 besser
big 8/3 groß
bill AE 13/9 Geldschein
black 5/4 schwarz
blue 5/3 blau
boarding card 7/1 Bordkarte
boarding pass 7/1 Bordkarte
boarding time 7/1 Einsteigezeit
book 2/1 Buch
bookshop 2/1 Buchhandlung
both 3/6 beide
bottle 3/1 Flasche
boy 4/2 Junge
breakfast 11/8 Frühstück
Britain 5/2 Britannien
British 5/2 britisch, Brite/Britin

brother **14/1** Bruder
brown **5/4** braun
building **10/2** Gebäude
bus **8/1** Bus
bus stop **10/2** Bushaltestelle
but **3/6** aber
buy **13/3** kaufen
bye **2/4** tschüs

C

café **2/1** Café
cake **4/2** Torte, Kuchen
can **6/3** können
car **2/1** Auto
car park **2/1** Parkplatz, Parkhaus, Tiefgarage
cashmere **13/3** Kaschmir, Kaschmirwolle
cathedral **8/5** Dom, Kathedrale
centre **8/3** Zentrum
check **1/4** Überprüfung, Kontrolle
check **6/3** überprüfen, kontrollieren
check-in **2/1** Abfertigung(sschalter), Check-in
Cheers! **3/** Prost!
cheese **4/2** Käse
cheesecake **4/2** Käsekuchen
childhood **9/8** Kindheit
chips **11/3** Pommes frites
chocolate **4/1** Schokolade
choir **12/2** Chor
church **8/5** Kirche
cinema **8/5** Kino
city **8/3** Stadt
class **12/2** Kurs
clothes (pl) **13/3** Kleider, Kleidung
coffee **4/1** Kaffee
Cologne **1/8** Köln
colour **5/3** Farbe
come **9/8** kommen
comfort **9/8** Komfort
company **15/1** Firma, Unternehmen
consolidation **5/** Vertiefung, Festigung

cook **12/2** kochen
cook **14/3** Koch/Köchin
cookery **12/2** Kochen
cookery programme **12/2** Kochsendung
cost **13/3** kosten
credit card **7/3** Kreditkarte
cup **4/2** Tasse

D

dance **12/2** tanzen
dancing **12/1** Tanzen
date **7/1** Datum
daughter **14/1** Tochter
day **3/4** Tag
Dear … **9/2** Liebe/r …
dialogue **1/3** Gespräch, Dialog
dinner **11/8** Abendessen
do **8/3** tun, machen
dot **6/9** Punkt
downtown **15/1** in der/die Innenstadt
drink **4/1** Getränk
drink **11/3** trinken
drive **15/1** fahren
duty-free **2/1** zollfrei

E

east **1/8** Osten
eat **11/1** essen
eight **4/9** acht
England **1/3** England
English **5/2** englisch, Engländer/in
enjoy **11/** genießen
Enjoy your meal! **11/** Guten Appetit!
euro **13/1** Euro
evening **11/9** Abend
evening class **12/2** Abendkurs
every **15/1** jede/r/s
Excuse me. **7/3** Entschuldigung!
eye **10/1** Auge

F

family **15/3** Familie
famous **10/2** berühmt

far 8/1 weit (entfernt)
father 14/1 Vater
fill in 5/6 ausfüllen, ergänzen
film 12/8 Film
fine 3/4 gut, schön
first name 6/9 Vorname
five 4/9 fünf
five-seater 9/8 Fünfsitzer
flag 5/3 Flagge
flight 7/ Flug
flight attendant 14/3 Flugbegleiter/in
food 11/3 Essen
football 13/11 Fußball
footballer 14/3 Fußballspieler/in
football shirt 13/11 Fußballtrikot
for 4/2 für
for lunch 11/8 zum Mittagessen
four 4/2 vier
free 12/2 frei
free time 12/2 Freizeit
Friday 10/9 Freitag
friend 10/11 Freund/in
friendly 9/2 freundlich
from 1/3 aus
fruit 13/8 Obst, Früchte

G

gallery 8/10 Galerie, Museum
game 13/3 Spiel
garden 10/2 Garten, Park
gardening 12/1 Gärtnern, Gartenarbeit
gate 2/1 Flugsteig, Gate
German 1/3 Deutsche/r, deutsch, Deutsch
Germany 1/3 Deutschland
girl 4/2 Mädchen
glass 3/ Glas
go 2/4 gehen
good 1/ gut
goodbye 2/4 auf Wiedersehen
Good to meet you! 1/ Schön, Sie/ dich/euch kennen zu lernen!
Go on. 11/3 Komm schon!
granddaughter 14/1 Enkelin

grandfather 14/1 Großvater
grandmother 14/1 Großmutter
grandson 14/1 Enkel
great 3/6 toll, prima, großartig
Great Britain 1/3 Großbritannien
green 5/4 grün
grey 5/4 grau
group 9/8 Gruppe
gym 10/2 Fitnessstudio

H

half past six 9/10 halb sieben
have sth 9/1 etw essen, etw trinken, etw (zu sich) nehmen
have 6/3 haben
he 2/4 er
hello 1/1 hallo
her 7/2 ihr
here 1/3 hier
Here you are. 3/1 Bitte (schön)., Hier, bitte.
hi 1/1 hallo
his 7/2 sein
home 6/3 Heim, Zuhause, Haus, Wohnung
hospital 10/2 Krankenhaus
hot 11/8 heiß, warm
hotel 2/1 Hotel
hour 9/8 Stunde
how 3/4 wie
how 13/ wie
How are you? 3/4 Wie geht es dir/euch/Ihnen?
How much is/are …? 13/ Wieviel kostet/n …?
hundred 13/10 hundert
hungry 4/2 hungrig
husband 12/2 (Ehe-)Mann

I

I 1/1 ich
I'm fine. 3/4 Mit geht es gut.
I'm = I am 1/1 ich bin

idea **8/3** Gedanke, Idee
in **1/3** in
information **2/1** Auskunft, Information(en)
in one day **9/2** innerhalb eines Tages, an einem (einzigen) Tag
interesting **8/3** interessant
in the evening **11/9** am Abend, abends
Ireland **1/3** Irland
Irish **2/4** irisch, Ire/Irin
I see. **14/3** Verstehe., Ah ja.
it **1/3** es
It doesn't say. **13/1** Das steht hier nicht.
It says … **13/1** Hier steht …

J

job **7/8** Arbeit, Stelle
juice **3/1** Saft
just **14/3** nur, gerade
Just a minute. **14/3** Moment mal., Einen Moment.

K

kindergarten teacher **14/3** Kindergärtner/in
know **13/1** wissen

L

lady **11/3** Dame
language **1/5** Sprache
let **6/** lassen
lift **2/1** Aufzug, Fahrstuhl, Lift
like **8/** wie
like **11/1** mögen
listen **1/1** zuhören
listening **2/9** Zuhören
little **4/2** klein
live **13/3** leben, wohnen
look **13/3** aussehen
love **12/2** lieben, sehr mögen
lovely **13/3** hübsch, nett, wunderbar

lunch **11/3** Mittagessen
lunchtime **11/3** Mittagszeit
luxury **9/8** Luxus

M

ma'am **13/10** gnädige Frau
magical **9/8** magisch, traumhaft
magic word **4/2** Zauberwort
main **11/8** Haupt-
man **3/8** Mann
many **8/3** viele
married to sb **14/3** mit jdm verheiratet
me **3/6** ich, mir, mich
meal **11/** Mahlzeit, Essen
meat **11/1** Fleisch
meet sb **1/** jdn treffen, jdm begegnen, jdn kennen lernen
meet sb **12/1** sich mit jdm treffen
menu **11/3** Speisekarte
Me too. **3/6** Ich auch.
mile **15/1** Meile
milk **4/2** Milch
miss **14/3** vermissen
mobile **6/3** Mobiltelefon, Handy
modern **8/10** modern
Monday **10/9** Montag
more **9/8** mehr
morning **12/10** Morgen
mother **14/1** Mutter
much **7/3** viel
Munich **1/8** München
museum **8/5** Museum
must **2/4** müssen
my **1/1** mein
mystery tour **9/8** Entdeckungsreise, Fahrt ins Blaue

N

name **1/1** Name
national **10/1** national, National-
near **1/3** in der Nähe von, nahe
new **1/3** neu
nice **2/4** schön, nett, gut

night 12/10 Abend, Nacht
nine 4/9 neun
no 1/3 nein
normal 8/3 normal, gewöhnlich
north 1/8 Norden
Northern Ireland 1/3 Nordirland
not 2/6 nicht
note BE 13/9 Geldschein
now 1/2 jetzt
number 5/3 Nummer

O

o'clock 9/10 Uhr
of 3/ von, aus
of course 6/3 natürlich, selbstverständlich
office 15/1 Büro
often 15/1 oft
old 9/2 alt
on 7/2 auf, an, bei
one 4/2 ein/e, eins
only 13/10 nur
only 14/3 erst
on the waterfront 9/1 am Wasser, im Hafen
on Thursday 10/10 am Donnerstag
open 10/10 offen, geöffnet
or 2/4 oder
orange 3/1 orange, Apfelsine
orange 5/4 orange
other 8/10 andere/r/s
our 9/8 unser
out of sth 8/3 außerhalb von etw

P

Pardon? 7/3 Wie bitte?
parents (pl) 15/1 Eltern
partner 14/1 Partner/in, Lebensgefährte/-in
passenger 7/1 Passagier
passport 7/1 Reisepass
past 9/10 nach
pence (pl) 13/9 Pence

people (pl) 9/2 Personen, Menschen, Leute
perfect 13/3 perfekt
person 8/3 Person, Mensch
phone 6/1 Telefon
photo 14/3 Foto
piece 4/2 Stück
pilot 14/3 Pilot/in
pink 5/4 rosa
place 3/6 Ort
play 12/1 spielen
please 3/ bitte
pm 10/10 nach 12 mittags
point 14/10 Punkt
policeman 14/3 Polizist
postcode 6/3 Postleitzahl
post office 8/5 Postamt
pound 13/9 Pfund
practice 1/6 Praxis, Übung, Training
present 13/3 Geschenk
price 9/8 Preis
programme 12/2 Sendung
pronunciation 1/10 Aussprache
pub 2/1 Kneipe
purple 5/4 lila, violett

Q

quick 1/4 schnell

R

read 7/2 lesen
real 13/3 echt
really 11/1 wirklich, tatsächlich
reception 2/1 Empfang, Rezeption
red 3/ rot
red wine 3/ Rotwein
relaxing 12/2 entspannend
repeat 1/1 wiederholen
restaurant 2/1 Restaurant
restaurant 8/5 Restaurant
retired 15/1 im Ruhestand
right 6/1 richtig

roast beef 11/3 Rinderbraten
round up 1/11 Zusammenfassung

S

Saturday 10/9 Samstag
say 6/3 sagen
science 10/1 Naturwissenschaft
Scotland 1/3 Schottland
seat 7/1 Platz, Sitz
secretary 15/1 Sekretär/in
see 2/4 sehen
see sth 9/1 etw besichtigen
See you again. 2/4 auf Wiedersehen
self service 4/1 Selbstbedienung
sell 13/3 verkaufen
seven 4/9 sieben
she 2/5 sie
shirt 13/11 Hemd
shop 2/1 Laden, Geschäft
shop assistant 7/3 Verkäufer/in
shopping centre 8/3 Einkaufszentrum
sight 10/2 Sehenswürdigkeit
sign 7/3 unterschreiben
sing 12/ singen
sir 7/3 mein Herr
's = is 1/1 ist
sister 14/1 Schwester
six 4/9 sechs
size 13/3 Größe
snack 4/1 Imbiss
so 4/2 also
soccer 13/3 Fußball
sometimes 15/1 manchmal
son 14/ Sohn
sorry 2/4 Entschuldigung!, Tut mir Leid!
soup 11/3 Suppe
south 1/8 Süden
spell 6/9 buchstabieren
sport 14/10 Sport
sports 12/9 Sport
student 3/3 Schüler/in
Sunday 10/9 Sonntag
sure 7/3 sicher

surname 6/3 Nachname
sweater 13/3 Pullover
swimming 12/1 Schwimmen
swimming pool 8/5 Schwimmbad
Swiss 5/2 schweizerisch, Schweizer/in
Switzerland 1/8 Schweiz

T

take 9/2 nehmen
taxi-cab 9/8 Taxi
tea 4/1 Tee
teacher 3/3 Lehrer/in
team 14/10 Mannschaft
ten 4/9 zehn
thanks 3/4 danke
thank you 4/2 danke
thank you very much 7/3 vielen Dank
that 3/6 der, die, das, diese/r/s, jene/r/s
That's right. 6/1 Das stimmt, Das ist richtig.
the 1/3 der, die, das
theatre 8/3 Theater
their 9/2 ihr/e
then 4/5 dann
there 3/6 dort, da
there is/are 8/1 es gibt
they 3/6 sie
thing 8/3 Ding, Sache
think 11/3 denken, glauben, finden
this 2/ diese/r/s, dies, das
three 4/2 drei
Thursday 10/9 Donnerstag
time 7/1 Zeit
to 1/ zu
to 7/3 nach
to 9/10 vor
to be hungry 4/2 Hunger haben
today 3/4 heute
to go for a walk 9/1 spazieren gehen
to go shopping 9/1 einkaufen gehen
toilet 2/1 Toilette
to keep in touch 6/ in Verbindung bleiben

too 3/6 auch, noch dazu
too 13/3 zu
too much 13/3 zu viel
top 10/1 oberste/r/s, Spitzen-
tour 8/3 Rundfahrt
tower 10/1 Turm
town 8/ Stadt
toy 13/11 Spielzeug
traditional 11/3 traditionell
train 8/1 Zug
Tuesday 10/9 Dienstag
tuna fish 15/10 Thunfisch
TV 12/1 Fernseher, Fernsehen
two 4/2 zwei

U

understand 9/2 verstehen

V

vegetarian 11/1 Vegetarier/in
very 3/6 sehr
Vienna 1/8 Wien
visit 9/1 besuchen, besichtigen

W

waiter 11/3 Kellner
waitress 1/3 Kellnerin
Wales 1/3 Wales
walk 9/1 Spaziergang
walking 12/1 Spazierengehen
want 13/3 wollen
watch 12/1 sehen, ansehen
watch TV 12/1 fernsehen
water 3/1 Wasser
waterfront 9/1 Hafen, Hafenviertel
we 3/6 wir
Wednesday 10/9 Mittwoch
weekend 12/10 Wochenende
welcome 7/3 willkommen

welcome to sb/sth 9/8 willkommen bei jdm/etw
well 10/3 nun, nun ja
west 1/3 Westen
What about …? 10/3 Wie wäre es mit …?
What about you? 4/2 Was ist mit dir/euch/Ihnen?
What colour is …? 5/3 Welche Farbe hat …?
what else? 8/3 was noch?
What time is it? 9/11 Wieviel Uhr ist es?, Wie spät ist es?
when 12/2 wann
where 1/3 wo
where 12/2 wohin
white 3/1 weiß
who 14/3 wer
why 11/3 warum
wife 14/1 (Ehe-)Frau
wine 3/ Wein
wish 9/2 Wunsch
with 6/9 mit
woman 3/4 Frau
word 1/8 Wort
work 12/2 Arbeit
work 14/3 arbeiten
would 13/3 würde

Y

yellow 5/4 gelb
yes 1/3 ja
you 1/2 du, ihr, dich, dir, euch
you're right 13/3 du hast Recht
You're welcome. 7/3 Bitte sehr., Gern geschehen.
you're = you are 1/3 du bist, ihr seid, Sie sind
your 6/1 dein, euer, Ihr

Names, places, countries and nationalities

EP = Extra Practice
FF = Facts & Fun
Film = Video auf DVD

Adam ['ædəm] 15/6
(the) Albert Dock ['ælbət dɒk] 10/Film 6
Alice ['ælɪs] 1/EP 2
America [ə'merɪkə] 13/6
Angela ['ændʒələ] 7/8
Atlanta [ət'læntə] 16/9
Australia [ɒ'streɪliə] 2/4
Australian [ɒ'streɪliən] 5/2
Austria ['ɒstriə] 1/8
Austrian ['ɒstriən] 5/2
(The) Beatles ['biːtlz] 1/FF
Becky ['beki] 5/1
Belgium ['beldʒəm] 5/1
Ben [ben] 1/EP 3
Bianca [bɪ'æŋkə] 15/6
Bill [bɪl] 4/2
Bill Shankly [ˌbɪl 'ʃæŋkli] 5/Film 3
Brandon ['brændən] 5/1
Brett [bret] 5/1
Brian [braɪən] 3/EP 6
Bridget ['brɪdʒɪt] 3/Film 1
Brighton ['braɪtn] 5/1
Britain ['brɪtn] 5/2
British ['brɪtɪʃ] 5/2
Burr [bɜː] 7/Film 4
(the) Cavendish Hotel [ˌkævəndɪʃ həʊ'tel] 10/2
(The) Cavern ['kævən] 9/8
Charlie ['tʃɑːli] 2/EP 4
Chessie ['tʃesi] 4/Film 2
Chicago [ʃɪ'kɑːgəʊ] 15/5
Chinese [tʃaɪ'niːz] 11/FF
Cologne [kə'ləʊn] 1/8
(the) Corinthia Hotel [kəˌrɪnθiə həʊ'tel] 10/2
Cork [kɔːk] 5/1

Czech Republic [ˌtʃek rɪ'pʌblɪk] 5/1
Dallas ['dæləs] 7/EP 6
Darwin ['dɑːwɪn] 3/6
David ['deɪvɪd] 1/EP 2
Denmark ['denmɑːk] 5/1
Denzel ['denzɪl] 12/1
Dublin ['dʌblɪn] 3/EP 6
Elizabeth [ɪ'lɪzəbəθ] 9/Film 5
Eltringham ['eltrɪŋəm] 12/Film 7
Emily ['emɪli] 3/EP 6
Emma ['emə] 1/EP 1
England ['ɪŋglənd] 1/3
English ['ɪŋglɪʃ] 5/2
European [ˌjʊərə'piːən] 15/Film 9
Everton ['evətən] 5/Film 3
Finn [fɪn] 15/6
Florida ['flɒrɪdə] 12/3
Forthlin Road [ˌfɔːθlɪn 'rəʊd] 10/Film 6
France [frɑːns] 5/1
Gatwick ['gætwɪk] 7/FF
George [dʒɔːdʒ] 10/Film 6
Georgina [ˌdʒɔː'dʒiːnə] 12/Film 7
German ['dʒɜːmən] 1/3
Germany ['dʒɜːməni] 1/3
Gloria ['glɔːriə] 3/EP 6
Gordon ['gɔːdn] 6/12
Graham Clarke [ˌgreɪəm 'klɑːk] 7/Film 4
Great Britain [ˌgreɪt 'brɪtn] 1/3
Harry ['hæri] 12/3
Heathrow ['hiːθrəʊ] 7/FF
Helen ['helən] 1/EP 5
Henry ['henri] 7/EP 3
Hungary ['hʌŋgəri] 5/1
Hyde Park [ˌhaɪd 'pɑːk] 10/1

Indian ['ɪndiən] 11/FF
Ireland ['aɪələnd] 1/3
Irish ['aɪrɪʃ] 2/4
Italian [ɪ'tæljən] 11/FF
Jack [dʒæk] 15/6
Jenny ['dʒeni] 12/Film 7
Jessica ['dʒesɪkə] 15/1
John Lennon [ˌdʒɒn 'lenən] 1/FF
Jordan ['dʒɔːdn] 6/12
Kansas ['kænzəs] 15/1
Kent [kent] 9/Film 5
Kerry ['keri] 2/EP 5
Kyla ['kaɪlə] 14/EP 2
Leeds Castle [ˌliːdz 'kɑːsl] 3/Film 1
Lime Street ['laɪm striːt] 5/Film 3
Limerick ['lɪmərɪk] 3/EP 6
Lisa ['liːsə] 5/EP 2
Liverpool ['lɪvəpuːl] 1/3
Lottie ['lɒti] 4/Film 2
Lucy ['luːsi] 1/EP 3
Luton ['luːtən] 7/FF
Luxembourg ['lʌksəmbɜːg] 5/1
Maidstone ['meɪstən] 14/Film 8
Manchester ['mæntʃɪstə] 2/EP 3
Marden ['mɑːdn] 3/Film 1
Maria [mə'riə] 5/1
Mary ['meəri]] 1/1
Mersey ['mɜːsi] 9/FF
Mexican ['meksɪkən] 11/FF
Miami [maɪ'æmi] 15/5
Munich ['mjuːnɪk] 1/8
Nairobi [naɪ'rəʊbi] 7/EP 6
(the) Netherlands ['neðələndz] 5/1
Newcastle ['njuːkɑːsl] 14/Film 8
Nick [nɪk] 3/Film 1
Nicole [nɪ'kəʊl] 14/3
Northern Ireland [ˌnɔːðən 'aɪələnd] 1/3
Olivia [ə'lɪviə] 5/1
Paris ['pærɪs] 12/8
Paul [pɔːl] 7/1
Paul McCartney [ˌpɔːl mə'kɑːtni] 10/Film 6
Paula ['pɔːlə] 4/2
Penny Lane [ˌpeni 'leɪn] 9/8

Perth [pɜːθ] 14/3
Peter ['piːtə] 13/EP 4
Poland ['pəʊlənd] 5/1
Qantas ['kwɒntəs] 14/3
Rachel ['reɪtʃəl] 3/Film 1
Ringo Starr [ˌrɪŋgəʊ 'stɑː] 10/Film 6
Rob [rɒb] 2/2
Rosa ['rəʊzə] 12/1
Sam [sæm] 14/3
(the) Savoy Hotel [səˌvɔɪ həʊ'tel] 10/2
Scotland ['skɒtlənd] 1/3
Sean Harvey [ˌʃɔːn 'hɑːvi] 3/Film 1
Sethi ['seθi] 14/EP 8
Sheffield ['ʃefiːld] 5/10
Sissinghurst ['sɪsɪŋhɜːst] 9/Film 5
Slovenia [sləʊ'viːniə] 5/1
Smith [smɪθ] 7/EP 3
Sophie ['səʊfi] 3/Film 1
St Paul's Cathedral [snt ˌpɔːlz kə'θiːdrəl] 10/1
Stansted ['stænsted] 7/FF
Susan ['suːzən] 4/EP 5
Susie ['suːzi] 4/2
Swiss [swɪs] 5/2
Switzerland ['swɪtsələnd] 1/8
Sydney ['sɪdni] 2/4
Tampa ['tæmpə] 15/1
Tina ['tiːnə] 14/3
Tom Jones [ˌtɒm 'dʒəʊnz] 6/FF
Toronto [tə'rɒntəʊ] 7/EP 6
Tunbridge ['tʌnbrɪdʒ] 3/Film 1
Tunbridge Wells [ˌtʌnbrɪdʒ 'welz] 4/Film 2
Tyler ['taɪlə] 15/4
(the) Unicorn ['juːnɪkɔːn] 12/Film 7
Vanessa [və'nesə] 5/EP 2
Vienna [vi'enə] 1/8
Wales [weɪlz] 1/3
Warrington ['wɒrɪŋtən] 1/3
Waters ['wɔːtəz] 10/11
Wichita ['wɪtʃɪtɔː] 15/1
William Shakespeare [ˌwɪljəm 'ʃeɪkspɪə] 7/Film 4
Wilson ['wɪlsən] 7/EP 5